# Silly Nana
# Does a Dance

by Stacey Roberts

Copyright 2023
All Rights Reserved.

# For Selah and Josie

Can you find the  ?

One day our silly Nana
left her home in Arizona
and parked her van
(that she named Vanna)
right on top of
Mom's begonias.

We were sitting on our front porch
the morning she arrived.
She popped right out of Vanna,

"Yoohoo!

It's me!

Surprise!"

She came walking up to greet us,
two steps forward, one step back,
her arms bent up beside her,
fingers going snap, snap, snap!

When she stepped up on the porch we could hear that she was saying, "Cha, cha, cha! Cha, cha, cha!" while her hips were swaying.

"Now you two come and join me!"
Nana jumped into the yard.
"Cha, cha, cha! Cha, cha, cha!
See dancing's not so hard!"

Cha!

Cha!

Cha!

We danced till we were tired,
then fell down laughing in the grass.
Our neighbor, Mildred, stopped to wave
as she was walking past.
Nana called out to her,
"Dance whenever there's a chance!"
One thing about our Nana,
she likes to do a dance.

We followed Nana to her Vanna
where she gave us each some shoes.
We laced them snugly on our feet
while she put some on, too.
The shoes had metal plates
on the bottoms of their soles.
Our heels went clippity-clap!
Tippity-tap-tap went our toes!

tippity-tap-tap

clippity-clap

Nana was clacking her shoes real loud
like there was nothing to it!
"Tap, tap, shuffle and then ball change.
This is how you do it!"
Our legs were swinging wildly
and our feet were moving faster,
but Nana put us both to shame.
She was the tap dance master!

We all removed our shoes
and went inside to get a drink.
We said, "Hi," to Mom and Dad
who were standing by the sink.
Mama gave us smoothies
made of pineapple and banana.

**Then guess who put on a grass skirt and danced the Hula-ala-Nana?**

"Aloha-hee, Aloha-hay, Aloha,
swing your hips this way.
Your arms move slow,
a story to show.
Your hands, like the ocean,
ebb and flow."
We moved our bare feet gently
like we were listening to a drum,
swaying our hips and
hands like Nana.
(Where'd she get these
grass skirts from?)

# Later on that evening, Nana took us to a show

where a beautiful ballerina
did a dance up on her toes!

Early the next morning,
Nana said she had to leave.
So we got into a line,

C'mon, Pop!

Nana, Mama, Sis and me.
We grabbed our daddy's hand,
"Come and join us, Pop!"

I'm in!

**Then we danced our Nana to her van
doing the Bunny Hop!
Point and tap your right foot twice,
with your left foot do the same.**

hop, hop, hop

**Jump forward, jump backward,
then forward as you say,
'Hop, hop, hop!'
while you hop, hop, hop.
We could do this dance all day!**

hop, hop, hop

We hugged our sweet, ole Nana
and we wished that she could stay.
She gave us each a kiss and
said she'd come again some day.

She tightened her bandana and began to drive away...

back over Mom's begonias,
back to sunny Arizona,

where silly Nanas
wear red bandanas
and love to dance all day.

# The End

Cha, cha, cha!

Also by Stacey Roberts:

Silly Nana Sings a Song
Silly Nana Hosts Halloween
Silly Nana Meets Mr. Moose
Flapadoodle and Schnoink
Where the Watermelon Grows

Printed in Great Britain
by Amazon